ASIAN COOKBOOK 2021

DELICIOUS AND HEALTHY RECIPES OF THE FAR EAST TRADITION

MICHAEL PENG

Table of Contents

2. Externalize

It revolves around knowing and understanding how you feel and being patient with these feelings. It's about accepting the hurt that you feel but not clinging to it. Knowing that there will be better days, and right now, it is okay to let it all out.

3. Appropriate process

This is a necessary process to help you cope with the devastation because it allows you to make sure you are not obsessing over the breakup and your feelings. It comes in five steps:

➢ Admit the pain or anger
➢ Vent, and let it out to the people who are most supportive - or write about it.
➢ Determine your response to your emotions (are you going to sit here and feel sorry for yourself, or are you going to try to get up and take care of yourself today?)
➢ Stick to your goals, and your plan to recovering and making it through this first stage of devastation
➢ Forget it. Shift your thoughts to something else, something more positive. You can only learn to forget once the other steps are taken care of.

4. Distraction

Devastation will destroy your sense of accomplishment and hold you from doing things you used to enjoy. This stage in the process is to fight back - do the opposite of what you feel. So, if you feel like sitting in bed all day, get up and sit on the couch or go outside for the day. Distract your mind with telephone calls to loved ones, play

crosswords, exercise, write, draw, etc. Do something creative, and don't allow yourself to sit with this pain.

5. Maintain your schedule

Whatever your routine was before, continue with it. If it is hard to fully maintain a routine right now, just do a couple a day, then gradually increase your strength to move on to the next thing you used to do. For example, if you used to wake up and go for a run, come home, shower, get ready for work, go to work, come home and make dinner, then read a book. Start by just getting up and going for a light walk and having a brisk shower. Day by day, increase your routine to one more thing on that list.

6. Find a place that doesn't trigger you.

If your breakup consisted of them moving, and you are stuck with all the memories no matter where you look, consider moving or staying with a friend for a while. If you had to move, and it hurts to go out and see the places you guys walked or went on dates, avoid these places and find somewhere new to go. Just don't avoid it forever.

7. Give in to the need for closeness without sexual contact.

The fastest way to get through this stage is physical closeness. So, if you have a child, cuddle them; if you have a best friend, ask for lots of hugs. When you need a shoulder to cry on, reach out to someone you trust. Along with this physical closeness, bonding with people you trust is a bonus in this recovery.

8. Avoid all things sexual

Although physical closeness is essential for recovering from a narcissist breakup, sexual entanglement with someone can make things worse. If you haven't completely moved on, you may feel shame, guilt, and even more anger. We want to avoid this as much as possible.

Devastation is the first stage of recovery, and it may also be the hardest. However, when you make it through this stage, you can move on to start taking better care of yourself, which will make you feel good. In short, you must let your feelings sink in, don't fight them, take care of your well-being, and stay off the internet or forums (at least for now). The last thing you want to do is overwhelm yourself with research that reminds you of your narcissistic relationship.

Allow Yourself to Grieve

Believe it or not, crying and tears are beneficial to your recovery. Crying is scientifically proven to rid your body of stress. When you let your other emotions in, this also helps with the grieving process. However, if you hold your emotions in, you are making connections in your brain that suggest holding it in is a better solution and will actually cause more problems for you later. When people hold their tears and anger in, they never learn to release or let go. Instead, they teach themselves that it is okay to hold it in, which can result in an outburst later. Have you ever cried so hard, then after you get this foggy feeling, but it feels as though a weight has almost lifted? This is because you have relieved yourself of the tension or stress that you feel.

Chapter 15:

Complex Post-Trauma Stress Symptoms

P ost-traumatic stress disorder is a result of some type of traumatic event. You've probably heard about it associated with war veterans, but it can also be caused by physical assaults, rape, car accidents, or emotional abuse. Really, any kind of disturbing or upsetting event that occurs can result in PTSD, particularly if it overwhelms your ability to cope with what happened. What's more, women are twice as likely to suffer from PTSD, and they also experience a longer duration of symptoms and more sensitivity to any triggers that remind them of the event. PTSD, as you've probably commonly heard of it, happens after a single traumatic incident, but there is another form, called Complex PTSD or C-PTSD, that results from repeated trauma over months or years. This is the type of PTSD we'll be talking about, though both types of PTSD share similar symptoms and treatments.

The effects of C-PTSD can be drastic if left untreated, and aside from the mental health implications of the condition, it can also lead to physical health problems. You might suffer from headaches, stomach problems, and sexual dysfunction, among other things. What happens with C-PTSD is that you do not only remember what happened; it's as if you're back in the incident you endured. It's like you went back in time and are living through that moment again. Your body responds as if you are too, and in response to it, the body

produces the stress hormones that result in a whole range of physical, mental, and emotional symptoms.

C-PTSD in Women

Women who are suffering from the effects of C-PTSD often don't seek help, sometimes for years, and then, when they do, the condition is frequently misdiagnosed or missed altogether by the health professional. It is also not uncommon that the woman herself may not be aware of the problem.

Women tend to internalize their problems, and rather than look outward to their situation, they might just decide that what they're suffering from is just a product of their own personality, thoughts, and emotions. They don't realize that there is a concrete problem from which they're suffering. For that reason, it's important to understand the causes, symptoms, and treatments for this condition. It's hard, though, because there is still a stigma against most mental health disorders, and that's particularly true for women who suffer from PTSD following an assault or C-PTSD following years of emotional abuse. Moreover, women are frequently traumatized further by the professionals in whom they confide. They might be questioned about the veracity of what they're saying and their reaction to the situation.

Differences in PTSD and C-PTSD Between Men and Women

As with many diseases and conditions, there is a difference in how women experience C-PTSD compared to men. Women, for example, are more likely to experience depression and anxiety while also having more difficulty feeling and dealing with their emotions.

Additionally, they often avoid activities and things that remind them of what happened to them. Alternatively, men are more likely to turn to alcohol or drugs to mask their emotional response to trauma.

The key to treating C-PTSD is to be educated about how it can affect you. It is a treatable condition, but you first have to recognize that you have a problem. This can be difficult for women since they frequently feel a need to be perfect and are often reluctant to admit they have something that they perceive as a weakness. It's not just their perception either; women are constantly told they need to do it all and must do it well. That's an unrealistic expectation and can create rather intense pressure. Before we talk about some of the treatment options for C-PTSD, let's look at some of the more common symptoms for women and men.

C-PTSD Symptoms

For C-PTSD to be diagnosed, a patient must experience symptoms for at least a month, though they could be suffering for months or years before going for a diagnosis. Symptoms might not appear immediately, either. When they do, they can typically be categorized into three types:

1. Re-experiencing the trauma, which typically occurs in the form of intrusive and distressing recollections of a single event or multiple events. These recollections could come in nightmares or through flashbacks.

2. Emotional numbness and avoidance of places, people, or activities that remind the individual of what happened to them.

3. Increased arousal, which can result in difficulty concentrating or sleeping, as well as feeling jumpy and being easily irritated and angered.

Typically, the traumatic events that cause PTSD, in general, include exposure to actual or threatened death, serious injury, or sexual violation, but trauma also occurs with long-term emotional abuse, where the individual's fight or flight response was repeatedly stimulated, eventually resulting in complex-PTSD. In this situation, the brain doesn't distinguish between physical trauma and emotional trauma; it only reads your fear and responds accordingly. It also tends to read anxiety as fear and responds with a cascade of physiological responses, including the production of stress hormones. The chronic production of stress hormones has dramatic physical and emotional effects. It's also important to note that the threat or abuse doesn't have to be directed at the individual involved, and both kinds of PTSD can also result when someone witnesses a traumatic event or emotional abuse. The specific symptoms for a diagnosis in each of these general categories include the following:

Re-Experiencing the Trauma

Re-experiencing trauma can take the following forms:

- Spontaneous, recurrent, and involuntary memories of the traumatic event that intrude into an individual's consciousness. For example, experiencing a memory can happen when a trigger is perceived. In children, this might be seen in how they play. Their play may take the form of themes or aspects of the trauma they suffered.

- Recurrent and distressing dreams related to the traumatic event- This might mean dreaming specifically about the event, but it can also just be dreams that have a feeling similar to it. In children, this may take the form of dreams that don't have any recognizable content.

- Dissociative reactions—such as flashbacks—where the individual experiences the memory as if it were actually happening again- This typically causes the individual to become fully immersed in the flashback.

- Intense, prolonged psychological distress from being exposed to either internal or external triggers that symbolize the traumatic events.

- Specific physiological reactions to reminders of the trauma they suffered. For example, some individuals might become nauseated when stimulated by a reminder of what they suffered.

Avoidance of Distressing Memories

This is a more typical response for women and can be diagnosed based on the presence of two or more of the following symptoms:

- An incapability to recall certain significant aspects of the traumatic event that cannot be accounted for by a head injury, alcohol, or drugs.

- Persistent and often exaggerated negative beliefs or expectations about oneself, other people, or the world in

general. For example, the person might say, "I am bad," "No one can be trusted," or "The world is a dangerous place."

- Persistent feelings of self-blame or blaming others regarding what caused the consequences of the traumatic events

- Persistent feelings of fear, horror, anger, shame, or guilt

- Diminished interest in participating in significant activities

- Feeling detached or estranged from other people.

- A persistent inability to experience positive emotions

Changes in Arousal and Reactivity

This can occur in both men and women and can be diagnosed based on two or more of the following changes:

- Irritability and a marked increase in aggression

- Reckless or self-destructive behavior.

- Hypervigilance.

- An exaggerated startle response.

- Problems concentrating.

- Significant distress or impairment in social or occupational areas of functioning that cannot be attributed to the effects of medication, drugs, alcohol, or some kind of medical condition like a traumatic brain injury

Treatment Options for PTSD and C-PTSD

There are several treatment options available for both kinds of PTSD

that have been shown to be effective for helping women cope with their symptoms. These include both psychological and medication-based treatments. The first step in treating PTSD (either kind), however, is to diagnose the condition. To diagnose PTSD, your doctor will begin with a physical examination to check for any medical problems that might be related to your symptoms; this is to rule out the possibility that your symptoms are caused by other conditions and not PTSD. Once those physical ailments are ruled out, the doctor may refer you to a psychologist for an evaluation. That will involve talking about your symptoms and the events that likely produced them. Finally, the psychologist will make use of the diagnostic criteria listed in the Diagnostic and Statistical Manual of Mental Disorders (DSM-5).

A diagnosis requires that you were exposed to trauma either directly, as a witness, or through learning someone close to you was traumatized. Additionally, you might have been repeatedly exposed to graphic details of a traumatic event, as might be the case with first responders. Along with exposure to the trauma of some kind, your symptoms must have been persistent for more than one month, and they must create significant problems in your ability to function in the different areas of your life.

Normalizing involves the following:

- Recognizing and accepting that physical pain may be a symptom. People with either kind of PTSD can struggle with migraines, back pain, or stomach and digestive issues.

- Recognizing and accepting that flashbacks or nightmares might occur and that they can be triggered by sounds, smells, or even a phrase that someone else says.

- By normalizing the symptoms, it can help alleviate the patient's sense of guilt. The treatment is still a long process, but it begins with hope. The goals of the treatment program include helping you regain a sense of control over your life by utilizing the following strategies:

- Teaching skills to address the symptoms as they occur.

- Helping you think more positively about yourself, other people, and the world in general.

- Learning better coping strategies for symptoms.

- Treating other symptoms related to the traumatic experience, like depression, anxiety, or substance abuse.

Chapter 16:

Letting Go and Moving On

W hether or not you feel like you have been the victim of narcissistic abuse, being in a relationship with a narcissist is not without its challenges and may lead to an unhappy end, or rather, it could lead to you staying in it, even when it contradicts who you are as a person and your dreams and goals of successful relationships and a happy life. Whatever you are feeling at this moment as you read this book, letting go of your relationship may not feel like your first choice, and that's okay.

For some readers, there is no question that it is time to pack up and go. It all depends on a person's wants and needs and their ability to be honest with the truth of what is really going on in their marriage or partnership. It can take some time to understand the dynamics of your narcissistic partnership after you have identified that you are in one.

Moving forward can be a challenge, and many people will struggle with putting an end to this type of relationship, mainly due to the reality of narcissistic abuse and emotional manipulation. It really is about who you are, what your experience is, and what is going on right now to help you understand the best choice forward for you.

The following will help you identify when it might be good to leave a narcissistic relationship and how to put an end to it so that you don't keep coming back to it and repeating the same patterns repeatedly. A lot of that experience requires getting help and support and

eventually a period of recovery from the narcissistic relationship so that you don't end up with the same type of person again, repeating the patterns in an entirely new relationship.

When and How to End the Relationship

The time is right for you to leave if you have undergone any emotional, mental or physical abuse, if you have identified serious cycles of manipulation or narcissistic issues that never change, if you are sacrificing your own personal power, integrity, success, and desires, or if you feel like you are being taken advantage of on a regular basis to support someone else's fantasies of who they are. There are a lot of ways that narcissism from within your relationship can affect your quality of life, your personal views, your self-worth, and more, and it is not worth it to stick around hoping that your partner will change and be more what you need. They don't care about what you need. They will only ever care about what they need.

If you have tried for a long time to help your partner identify their issue and help them "heal" their problem to no avail, then it is time to let go and move on. It is important to recognize that you can never heal someone for them; they have to do the work to heal themselves. Being a supportive partner is always a good thing, but if you are familiar with how your patterns of support have enabled your narcissistic partner to stay in their preferred role and behavior patterns, then you need to admit that you are at the end of the rope so that you can heal on your own terms and find a happier lifestyle.

The stages of detaching from your partner can go on for a while as you begin to identify the issues and start to pull away, changing your role in the situation and recognizing your readiness to end things. It can

be uncomfortable for your partner, who will make it uncomfortable for you as a result, and so understanding some of the stages that you will likely go through will help you prepare for moving on.

Detachment from a Narcissist: Stages

First Stage:

When the rose-colored glasses come off, and you stop accepting blame, guilt, or shame in your relationship, you begin to resurface and "wake up" to what has really been going on. In the first stage, you are "seeing" more clearly all of the patterns, the covert and subversive ridicule, and all of the tools of manipulation to push you away and punish you, and then pull you back in and adore you. This is the stage of awareness of the problem and the first shift and change in the situation.

Second Stage:

You may still have feelings for your partner at this point, even a seriously deep love bond; however, your usual desire to please them no matter what will begin to be replaced with the feeling of anger and even resentment that they are so consistently and continuously demanding of your admiration, adoration and pleasing them. The love may still be there, but you are not so "naïve" anymore.

Signals of the Second Stage:

- Your partner's lies no longer have an effect on you and feel obvious and pathetic.

- You are no longer succumbing to the manipulation tools.

- You regain a sense of self-worth and feel you deserve to be treated better.

- You begin to fight for yourself more and create more conflict with your partner.

- You begin to regain and rebuild your self-confidence and self-esteem.

Third Stage:

Your confidence is being reborn, and you feel better about yourself and your choices. You may have already joined a support group at this time or started to see a counselor to help with your growth and are feeling more empowered emotionally and mentally. You can better focus on your own wants and needs and start seeing how life would be if you are not involved with your narcissistic partner.

Signals of the third stage:

- You cannot stand to be around your partner.

- You no longer feel an obsessive love or strong love bond.

- If they begin to push your buttons or act inappropriately, you will either have no reaction and not care or retaliate and lash out against them.

- Enjoy more time with friends, in support groups, engage in classes or group meet-ups that support your interests

- You will start to make decisions to support yourself without concerning yourself with your partner's preferences or interests.

- You will begin to make your move to let go and move on by planning your out and getting your ducks in a row.

Fourth Stage:

This is the end of the relationship when your focus becomes facing your future without your partner. At this point, you may have cut the cords, moved out, separated, begun the divorce proceedings, etc. This is the stage when you will have cut them off and out of your life and when you can begin to feel new and like yourself again. You will not want anything to do with your partner, and in some cases, you may have to maintain some kind of contact (if you have children together).

The Overall Process of Letting Go and Moving On:

This process won't occur for anyone overnight. You can end up living in the cycle of one stage for a long time until you are resolved to move forward into the next stage. Being stuck in these processes is highly common, and there is a way to help you ease through a little bit better so that you don't stay stuck for longer than you need to be.

As you begin to consider letting go and moving on, hang onto those thoughts and let yourself feed into them. You are allowed to imagine your life differently, apart from your partner, and it can help you to build steam and momentum if you continually consider the process of cutting cords and stepping forward. It helps to keep fueling your self-esteem and doing things that will help you support yourself in the process. Follow these steps to help:

1. Think about it. Let yourself fuel your exit with self-esteem building and thoughts about moving on. Build momentum so

that you can keep revisiting why you are having these thoughts to begin with.

2. Use a journal or a notebook to write out all of the experiences you want to have, the life you want to live, the places you want to go, and where you want to be successful in your life. Start to write down and consider the kind of partnership and partner you would like to experience. You can even jot down all of the aspects of your current relationship and then make a comparison between what you have and what you really want. Getting into the habit of journaling about you and what you want can help you refocus your life goals and ambitions and further motivate you to let go of the relationship that is hurting your choices and chances for a healthy and successful life.

3. Reflect. Explore your relationship and ask yourself what part, or role, you have played in the experience. The narcissist may be manipulative, toxic, and cunning, but it certainly always takes two to tango, and so it might help you to be honest and identify what ways you have supported the toxicity of your relationship. How have you not lived up to your own standards of love and life? How have you enabled this behavior? What can you do to shift these patterns? Spend time with these thoughts and truly reflect on your own energy in the relationship. Write it down in your journal and begin to create awareness about your role in the partnership. You don't want to fall for the narcissist again, and knowing where you fall for the traps can help you resist them in the future.

4. Find supportive literature. There are countless books out there that aren't just about overcoming a narcissistic relationship, but that are also about empowering yourself, finding the career of your dreams, learning new skills and hobbies, and so on. You can begin to reclaim your identity and your sense of pride and joy in your life by seeking out self-improvement books and literature that will empower you and give you strength.

5. Spend time with others. Connect with your family, friends, co-workers, support groups, etc., and talk about it. Feel free to be yourself around your network of loving and supportive people to help you feel that you are not going to be alone when you walk away and move forward.

Chapter 17:

Maintaining a Healthy Relationship

I f you are already in an unbalanced relationship and want it to change, check out some of these tips.

Take A Good Look At The Relationship

Is it worth pursuing? Is it unbalanced because you no longer love and respect each other? Is it because you've grown apart?

In addition to answering those questions, you have to recognize that certain behaviors like:

- Swearing or yelling at you

- Harassing statements that are directed toward you

- Interrogating or degrading you in any way

- Attacking your self-esteem and that of your loved ones

- Blaming you for the things that go wrong in his or her life (or in general)

- Extreme jealousy

- Gaslighting

- Threatening you in any way (specifically physical or sexual abuse)

- Threats to your family members or friends

- Threats to your kids or pets

- Controlling behavior

- Isolating you from your loved ones

- Controlling you with money or any other means

are not healthy.

Be Clear & Honest With One Another

If you want something to change, you can't lie to the other person or hold in your feelings. You have to offer up your feelings and allow your partner the same respect. Use "I statements": "I feel that..." "This behavior makes me feel that I..."

Not only that, offer up examples of why you feel this way. Don't just give him or her general statements. The more specific, the more of a chance that you'll get a positive change

Consider The Option of "Miscommunication"

Sometimes, things are not how we perceive them to be. If you think that your partner isn't being considerate because he isn't texting you back when you ask questions or because you always have to come up with the plan of action, consider this:

He might just be clueless. I'm not making excuses for your partner. I'm just urging you to be communicative and open-minded. It could just be a horrible, horrible case of miscommunication.

Keep In Mind That We Shouldn't "Change" People

We can't change anyone. They have to be willing to change themselves. You can't force someone to act the way that you want – especially adults. We can change the way we do things, and we can

express how we feel and what we need. However, it is up to your partner what he or she wants to do with that information.

Try To Restore Balance To Yourself First

We have to treat ourselves with respect before we expect others to respect us. This is a statement that we often take for granted. We expect others to immediately be respectful toward us, but we don't take care of ourselves.

Reflection is an important step in fixing any relationship. Look within yourself to find what you can do to be happy. Listen to your instincts and trust them. Be open to what your reflection reveals about you and what you need. Find healthy stress relief techniques and treat your body right. These things will lead to a happier life and will lead you to a happy relationship.

Insecurity and Jealousy

Some people may say that the reason for their behavior is insecurity and jealousy. This is not an excuse for treating anyone in a cruel or abusive manner. However, if you deal with insecurity and jealousy at their roots, you can control those behaviors. Counseling will help with these, but there are some things that you can do at home. The first step is to recognize insecurity and jealousy.

Insecurity is a lack of confidence or assurance. You can also call it self-doubt, anxiety, or a lack of confidence. If you are feeling insecure, there is more of a chance that you will develop unhealthy levels of jealousy while you are in a relationship.

There are many different types of people, and we all handle our insecurities in different ways. We can categorize most people into six

119

different categories based on how they handle what they view as their shortcomings:

- People who take those insecurities as a challenge (to better themselves so that they can overcome them),

- People that use humor as a defense mechanism,

- People who just surround themselves with positivity and pretend that they don't have any insecurities at all,

- People who lie about themselves in order to cover up any insecurities (I mean, outlandish wild tales!),

- People who verbally doubt themselves and put themselves down, and

- People who act out because of their insecurities in order to cover them up.

Most of us strive for the first category but end up falling into one of the latter ones. That doesn't mean that we can't change, though.

The Most Important Relationship That You Should Rescue

The most important relationship that should be mended after you leave an abusive relationship is your own relationship with yourself. You need to be able to fix the damage done to your self-esteem because of all of that emotional and mental abuse. Because of that, I want to talk about what you can do to build your confidence:

Self-confidence is a trait that we all take for granted. We rarely think about the ways that self-confidence helps us in our daily lives. One of the most important ways that it helps us is by helping us overcome our fears.

When we improve and build up our self-esteem and confidence level, it can really help us pursue our dreams. We will all fear certain things in our lives. Sometimes it is a phobia buried deep in our subconscious (fear of the unknown, the dark, clowns, being alone, etc.). Other times, we can easily overcome some of our fears by building up our strengths and by being confident in ourselves.

Let's talk about how we can do that. How we can build up that self-assurance so that we can be happy with ourselves is the first step to being happy with your life. Here are some simple steps that you can take to start that process. Mind you, you don't have to do these in any order.

Choose a couple off of the list to try first. If it doesn't work immediately, give them about a week to really have an effect. Keep up with the ones you feel most comfortable with, and drop the ones that aren't working for you. This is your life and your happiness. Do what feels good (and healthy) for you.

1.   Become a master at something.

Learning, practicing, and pursuing things that you feel passionate about helps to liberate your mind while focusing it on something specific. This practice will help you focus on other things as well. Practice makes perfect, right?

Studies have shown that it takes approximately 10,000 hours before we can master a specific skill. That is a lot of practicing and a lot of time to focus your mind on a specific task.

If you use this practice time with a task that inspires you, it is time well spent, and you will find it easier to focus. Don't know what

activity or skill to choose? Answer some of the questions below to help you zone in on what you feel passionate about:

- Are you a creative person? Do you like to create things with your hands?

- Have you always wanted to try a particular sport or physical activity?

- What hobbies do you enjoy doing when you are by yourself?

- Which of your skills are friends and family members always commenting on?

- Is there something that you enjoy doing, which you would also be inclined to create? For example, are you an avid reader? Would you like to try your hand at writing a book?

2. Play dress-up.

When you feel presentable, and when you dress nicely, you can feel like you're ready to take on the rest of the world. You don't have to go out and buy something expensive or fancy. Casual clothes can be presentable too. You have to find the balance between comfortable and well-dressed.

Creating your own sense of style can help increase your confidence level too. Bring out your personality in your clothes. Don't be afraid to think outside of the box – as long as it goes with the dress code at work. If you're not interested in being fashionable or focusing on your appearance at all, just keep in mind that it's not bad to be known for having a clean and professional appearance.

3. Create an image of how you picture yourself.

When people say that you should "dress for the job that you want, not the job that you have," what they mean is that you should create a self-image of success.

If you can and if you have the software, create an image on your computer. Place yourself in the position that you want to be in five years from now or fifteen years from now. These mental images that we have for success are great ways to motivate ourselves to work harder and work better. Making these mental images into visual and tangible images that you can reference every day will make you feel great.

4. Squash those negative thoughts.

Negativity is your worst enemy. Be aware of how you talk about yourself and how you think of yourself. Negative thoughts can be anything from "I want to quit this" to "I look and feel gross today." The first step to stopping negative thoughts is to recognize this type of self-talk.

The second step is to visualize yourself actively stopping these types of thoughts from entering your mind. You can picture anything that works for you, including (but not limited to):

- Picturing these thoughts as water and stopping them with a dam inside your head,

- Imagining these thoughts as bugs and squashing them with a big boot or a stiletto heel, and

- Visualizing these thoughts as cannonballs and shooting them far away.

Conclusion:

Emotional abuse can be every bit as damaging as physical abuse. In fact, the scars can last longer, and it can take longer to identify since there are many ways for a partner to be emotionally abusive. Often they will dress it up as care and concern, but, in fact, it's all about control. For whatever reason, they feel the need to control your life and destroy your self-esteem and question your own emotional health.

Many emotional abusers have suffered similar treatment at the hands of parents, friends, family, or colleagues, although not all abusers were themselves victims of emotional abuse. Whatever the reason for this behavior, it is not acceptable, and you do not have to tolerate it, although it can be very difficult to escape from, since the abuser may not even realize they have a problem, or if they do, they may be unwilling to change.

It is possible to recover from emotional abuse and be happy again, as long as you can let go of the past and decide on new boundaries and expectations for future relationships. You can be happy again – and indeed, you deserve to be!

As we end this book, I would like to reiterate some points in recovering from Emotional Abuse:

1. The first step is to recognize the problem and then find out as much information about emotional abuse as you can from books and the Internet.

2. Do not hesitate to seek help from a qualified counselor, therapist, or support group, and be prepared to ask a lot of questions.

3. It is imperative that you always tell your friends and family what is going on, even if they are not very sympathetic or understanding. If they do not know, others may expect them to know or be afraid they will become a victim of Emotional Abuse – especially children! The more evidence of the problem there is, the more likely it will be that someone else will take action on your behalf if you are still experiencing it by yourself.

4. Seek professional help if things do not improve, or your abuser becomes more aggressive as time goes on – which is often the case. Most abusive people are totally unaware of the damage they cause. If you tell them you want to make a change, it's not always easy for them (even if they are willing) to change their ways, especially without professional intervention and close supervision.

5. The same applies if you are still experiencing other forms of abuse at the same time as Emotional Abuse – it is not uncommon for perpetrators of all types of abuse to engage in more than one form at once, although there may be some differences in intensity and severity between the different types.

6. If you are still experiencing Emotional Abuse, there is no need to let it continue. Never be afraid to speak the truth about what is happening in your life, and never do anything that you

feel uncomfortable about or make you want to undo an action later on.

7. Do not give up: there's always hope.

Well, you have reached the end of our journey through this book – a journey that has helped hundreds of thousands of people recover from Emotional Abuse and get their lives back on track! I hope it has been helpful, and I wish you the very best in your recovery and future relationships.

CPSIA information can be obtained
at www.ICGtesting.com
Printed in the USA
BVHW091932270521
608295BV00001B/186

Introduction

Everyone who loves to cook, loves to experiment with new dishes and new taste sensations. Chinese cuisine has become immensely popular in recent years because it offers a different range of flavours to enjoy. Most dishes are cooked on top of the stove, and many are quickly prepared and cooked so are ideal for the busy cook who wants to create an appetising and attractive dish when there is little time to spare. If you really enjoy Chinese cooking, you will probably already have a wok, and this is the perfect utensil for cooking most of the dishes in the book. If you have yet to be convinced that this style of cooking is for you, use a good frying pan or saucepan to try out the recipes. When you find how easy they are to prepare and how tasty to eat, you will almost certainly want to invest in a wok for your kitchen.

Serves 4

10 dried Chinese mushrooms

225 g/8 oz asparagus

1 bunch spring onions (scallions), trimmed

600 ml/1 pt/2½ cups chicken stock

5 ml/1 tsp cornflour (cornstarch)

15 ml/1 tbsp water

5 ml/1 tsp salt

Soak the mushrooms in warm water for 30 minutes then drain. Discard the stalks. Arrange the mushrooms in the centre of a strainer then arrange the spring onions and asparagus in a circle radiating out from the centre. Bring the stock to the boil then lower the strainer into the stock, cover and simmer gently for about 10 minutes until the vegetables are just tender. Remove the vegetables and invert them on to a warmed serving plate to maintain the pattern. Bring the stock to the boil. Blend the water, cornflour and salt to a paste, stir it into the stock and simmer, stirring, until the sauce thickens slightly. Spoon over the vegetables and serve at once.

Asparagus Stir-Fry

Serves 4

45 ml/3 tbsp groundnut (peanut) oil

1 spring onion (scallion), chopped

450 g/1 lb asparagus

30 ml/2 tbsp soy sauce

5 ml/1 tsp sugar

120 ml/4 fl oz/½ cup chicken stock

5 ml/1 tsp cornflour (cornstarch)

Heat the oil and fry the spring onion until lightly browned. Add the asparagus and stir-fry for 3 minutes. Add the remaining ingredients and stir-fry for 4 minutes.

Sweet and Sour Asparagus

Serves 4

30 ml/2 tbsp groundnut (peanut) oil

450 g/1 lb asparagus, cut in diagonal pieces

60 ml/4 tbsp wine vinegar

50 g/2 oz/¼ cup brown sugar

15 ml/1 tbsp soy sauce

15 ml/1 tbsp rice wine or dry sherry

5 ml/1 tsp salt

15 ml/1 tbsp cornflour (cornstarch)

Heat the oil and stir-fry the asparagus for 4 minutes. Add the wine vinegar, sugar, soy sauce, wine or sherry and salt and stir-fry for 2 minutes. Mix the cornflour with a little water, stir it into the pan and stir-fry for 1 minute.

Aubergine with Basil

Serves 4

60 ml/4 tbsp groundnut (peanut) oil
2 aubergines (eggplants)
60 ml/4 tbsp water
2 cloves garlic, crushed
1 red chilli pepper, diagonally sliced
45 ml/3 tbsp soy sauce
1 large bunch basil

Heat the oil and fry the aubergine until lightly browned. Add the water, garlic, chilli pepper and soy sauce and stir-fry until the aubergine changes colour. Add the basil and stir-fry until the leaves are wilted. Serve at once.

Braised Aubergine

Serves 4

1 aubergine (eggplant)
oil for deep-frying
15 ml/1 tbsp groundnut (peanut) oil
3 spring onions (scallions), chopped
1 slice ginger root, chopped
90 ml/6 tbsp chicken stock
15 ml/1 tbsp rice wine or dry sherry
15 ml/1 tbsp soy sauce
15 ml/1 tbsp black bean sauce
15 ml/1 tbsp brown sugar

Peel the aubergine and cut it into large cubes. Heat the oil and deep-fry the aubergine until soft and lightly browned. Remove and drain well.

Heat the oil and fry the spring onions and ginger until lightly browned. Add the aubergine and stir well. Add the stock, wine or sherry, soy sauce, black bean sauce and sugar. Stir-fry for 2 minutes.

Serves 4

6 slices bacon

2 cloves garlic, crushed

2 spring onions (scallions), chopped

1 aubergine (eggplant), peeled and diced

4 tomatoes, skinned and quartered

salt and freshly ground pepper

Cut the rind off the bacon and cut into chunks. Fry until lightly browned. Add the garlic and spring onions and stir-fry for 2 minutes. Add the aubergine and stir-fry for about 5 minutes until slightly soft. Carefully mix in the tomatoes and season with salt and pepper. Stir gently over a low heat until heated through.

Steamed Aubergine

Serves 4

1 aubergine (eggplant)

30 ml/2 tbsp soy sauce

5 ml/1 tsp groundnut (peanut) oil

Score the aubergine skin a few times and place it in an ovenproof dish. Place on a rack in a steamer and steam over gently simmering water for about 25 minutes until soft. Leave to cool slightly then peel off the skin and tear the flesh into shreds. Sprinkle with soy sauce and oil and stir well. Serve hot or cold.

Stuffed Aubergine

Serves 4

4 dried Chinese mushrooms

225 g/8 oz minced (ground) pork

2 spring onions (scallions), minced

1 slice ginger root, minced

30 ml/2 tbsp soy sauce

15 ml/1 tbsp rice wine or dry sherry

5 ml/1 tsp sugar

1 aubergine (eggplant), halved lengthways

Soak the mushrooms in warm water for 30 minutes then drain. Discard the stalks and chop the caps. Mix with the pork, spring onions, ginger, soy sauce, wine or sherry and sugar. Scoop out the seeds of the aubergine to make a hollow shape. Stuff with the pork mixture and arrange in an ovenproof dish. Place on a rack in a steamer and steam over gently simmering water for 30 minutes until tender.

Stir-Fried Aubergine

Serves 4–6

4 dried Chinese mushrooms

1 aubergine (eggplant), peeled and diced

30 ml/2 tbsp cornflour (cornstarch)

oil for deep-frying

45 ml/3 tbsp groundnut (peanut) oil

50 g/2 oz cooked chicken, diced

50 g/2 oz smoked ham, diced

50 g/2 oz bamboo shoots, chopped

50 g/2 oz/½ cup chopped mixed nuts

5 ml/1 tsp salt

5 ml/1 tsp sugar

30 ml/2 tbsp soy sauce

30 ml/2 tbsp rice wine or dry sherry

Soak the mushrooms in warm water for 30 minutes then drain. Discard the stalks and slice the caps. Toss the aubergine lightly in cornflour. Heat the oil and deep-fry the aubergine until golden. Remove from the pan and drain well. Heat the oil and stir-fry the chicken, ham, bamboo shoots and nuts. Add the remaining ingredients and stir-fry for 3 minutes. Return the aubergine to the pan and stir-fry until heated through.

Serves 4

50 g/2 oz chicken meat, minced (ground)

50 g/2 oz smoked ham, minced (ground)

50 g/2 oz water chestnuts, minced (ground)

2 egg whites

15 ml/1 tbsp cornflour (cornstarch)

225 g/8 oz bamboo shoots, cut into thick strips

15 ml/1 tbsp chopped flat-leaved parsley

Mix together the chicken, ham and water chestnuts. Mix together the egg whites and cornflour then stir them into the minced ingredients. Stir the bamboo shoots into the mixture until well coated then arrange in an ovenproof dish. Place on a rack in a steamer, cover and steam over gently simmering water for 15 minutes. Serve garnished with parsley.

Deep-Fried Bamboo Shoots

Serves 4

oil for deep-frying

225 g/8 oz bamboo shoots, cut into strips

15 ml/1 tbsp groundnut (peanut) oil

15 ml/1 tbsp brown sugar

15 ml/1 tbsp soy sauce

10 ml/2 tsp cornflour (cornstarch)

90 ml/6 tbsp water

Heat the oil and deep-fry the bamboo shoots until golden. Drain well. Heat the groundnut (peanut) oil and stir-fry the bamboo shoots until coated with oil. Mix together the sugar, soy sauce, cornflour and water, stir into the pan and stir-fry until heated through.

Serves 4

90 ml/6 tbsp groundnut (peanut) oil

1 spring onion, cut into strips

1 clove garlic, crushed

1 red chilli pepper, cut into strips

225 g/8 oz bamboo shoots

15 ml/1 tbsp thick soy sauce

2.5 ml/½ tsp sesame oil

Heat the oil and stir-fry the spring onion, garlic and chilli pepper for 30 seconds. Add the bamboo shoots and stir-fry until just tender and well coated in the spices. Add the soy sauce and sesame oil and stir-fry for a further 3 minutes. Serve at once.

Bamboo Shoots with Mushrooms

Serves 4

8 dried Chinese mushrooms

45 ml/3 tbsp groundnut (peanut) oil

350 g/12 oz bamboo shoots, cut into strips

30 ml/2 tbsp soy sauce

5 ml/1 tsp brown sugar

15 ml/1 tbsp cornflour (cornstarch)

45 ml/3 tbsp water

Soak the mushrooms in warm water for 30 minutes then drain. Discard the stalks and slice the caps. Heat the oil and stir-fry the mushrooms for 2 minutes. Add the bamboo shoots and stir-fry for 3 minutes. Add the soy sauce and sugar and stir well until heated through. Transfer the vegetables to a warmed serving plate using a slotted spoon. Mix the cornflour and water to a paste and stir it into the pan. Simmer, stirring, until the sauce clears and thickens then pour it over the vegetables and serve at once.

Serves 4

6 dried Chinese mushrooms
250 ml/8 fl oz/1 cup chicken stock
15 ml/1 tbsp rice wine or dry sherry
15 ml/1 tbsp soy sauce
15 ml/1 tbsp groundnut (peanut) oil
225 g/8 oz bamboo shoots, sliced
15 ml/1 tbsp cornflour (cornstarch)

Soak the mushrooms in warm water for 30 minutes then drain. Discard the stems and slice the caps. Place the mushroom caps in a pan with half the stock, the wine or sherry and soy sauce. Bring to the boil, cover and simmer for about 10 minutes until thick. Add the oil and stir over a medium heat for 2 minutes. Add the bamboo shoots and stir-fry for 3 minutes. Mix the cornflour into the remaining stock and stir it into the pan. Bring to the boil, stirring, then simmer for about 4 minutes until the sauce thickens and clears.

Bamboo Shoots in Oyster Sauce

Serves 4

15 ml/1 tbsp groundnut (peanut) oil

350 g/12 oz bamboo shoots, cut into strips

250 ml/8 fl oz/1 cup chicken stock

15 ml/1 tbsp oyster sauce

5 ml/1 tsp soy sauce

2.5 ml/½ tsp brown sugar

2.5 ml/½ tsp sesame oil

Heat the oil and stir-fry the bamboo shoots for 1 minute. Add the stock, oyster sauce, soy sauce and sugar and bring to the boil. Simmer for about 10 minutes until the bamboo shoots are tender and the liquid has reduced. Serve sprinkled with sesame oil.

Bamboo Shoots with Sesame Oil

Serves 4

100 g/4 oz bean sprouts

45 ml/3 tbsp groundnut (peanut) oil

225 g/8 oz bamboo shoots

5 ml/1 tsp salt

5 ml/1 tsp sesame oil

Cook the bean sprouts in boiling water for about 10 minutes until tender but still crisp. Drain well. Meanwhile, heat the oil and stir-fry the bamboo shoots for about 5 minutes until tender but still crisp. Sprinkle with salt, mix well then arrange with the bean sprouts on a warmed serving plate. Sprinkle with sesame oil and serve.

Bamboo Shoots with Spinach

Serves 4

45 ml/3 tbsp groundnut (peanut) oil
450 g/1 lb bamboo shoots
5 ml/1 tsp rice wine or dry sherry
pinch of salt
120 ml/4 fl oz/½ cup chicken stock
100 g/4 oz spinach
2.5 ml/½ tsp sesame oil

Heat the oil and fry the bamboo shoots for about 1 minute. Add the wine or sherry, salt and stock, bring to the boil and simmer for 3 minutes. Add the spinach and simmer until the spinach has wilted and the liquid reduced slightly. Transfer to a warmed serving bowl and serve sprinkled with sesame oil.

Broad Bean Sauté

Serves 4

450 g/1 lb shelled broad beans

60 ml/4 tbsp groundnut (peanut) oil

5 ml/1 tsp salt

10 ml/2 tsp brown sugar

75 ml/5 tbsp chicken stock

salt

2 spring onions (scallions), chopped

Place the beans in a pan, just cover with water, bring to the boil and simmer until tender. Drain well.

Heat the oil then add the beans and stir until well coated with oil. Add the sugar and stock and season to taste with salt. Stir-fry for 3 minutes. Stir in the spring onions and serve.

Serves 4

45 ml/3 tbsp groundnut (peanut) oil

2 dried red chilli peppers

2 onions, chopped

450 g/1 lb green beans

Heat the oil with the chilli peppers and fry until they change colour then remove them from the pan. Add the onions and stir-fry until lightly browned. Meanwhile, blanch the beans in boiling water for 2 minutes then drain well. Add to the onions and stir-fry for 10 minutes until tender but still crisp and well coated in the spiced oil.

Spiced Green Beans

Serves 4

450 g/1 lb green beans
15 ml/1 tbsp salt
5 ml/1 tsp ground anise
5 ml/1 tsp freshly ground red pepper

Place all the ingredients in a large pan and just cover with water. Bring to the boil and simmer for about 8 minutes until the beans are just tender. Drain well before serving.

Stir-Fried Green Beans

Serves 4

45 ml/3 tbsp groundnut (peanut) oil
5 ml/1 tsp salt
450 g/1 lb string beans, cut into pieces
120 ml/4 fl oz/½ cup chicken stock
15 ml/1 tbsp soy sauce

Heat the oil and salt then add the beans and stir-fry for 2 minutes. Add the stock and soy sauce, bring to the boil, cover and simmer for about 5 minutes until the beans are tender but still slightly crisp.

Sautéed Bean Sprouts

Serves 4

15 ml/1 tbsp groundnut (peanut) oil

450 g/1 lb bean sprouts

15 ml/1 tbsp soy sauce

salt and freshly ground pepper

Heat the oil and stir-fry the bean sprouts for about 3 minutes. Add the soy sauce, salt and pepper and stir together well. Cover and simmer for 5 minutes then remove the lid and simmer for a further 1 minute.

Bean Sprout Stir-Fry

Serves 4

15 ml/1 tbsp groundnut (peanut) oil

2.5 ml/½ tsp salt

1 clove garlic, crushed

450 g/1 lb bean sprouts

3 spring onions (scallions), chopped

60 ml/4 tbsp chicken stock

5 ml/1 tsp sugar

5 ml/1 tsp soy sauce

Heat the oil, salt and garlic until the garlic turns light golden. Add the bean sprouts and spring onions and stir-fry for 2 minutes. Add the remaining ingredients and stir-fry for a few minutes until all the liquid has evaporated.

Bean Sprouts and Celery

Serves 4

450 g/1 lb bean sprouts

45 ml/3 tbsp groundnut (peanut) oil

4 stalks celery, cut into strips

5 ml/1 tsp salt

15 ml/1 tbsp soy sauce

90 ml/6 tbsp chicken stock

Blanch the bean sprouts in boiling water for 3 minutes then drain. Heat the oil and stir-fry the celery for 1 minute. Add the bean sprouts and stir-fry for 1 minute. Add the remaining ingredients, bring to the boil, cover and simmer for 3 minutes before serving.

Bean Sprouts and Peppers

Serves 4

225 g/8 oz bean sprouts

45 ml/3 tbsp groundnut (peanut) oil

2 dried chilli peppers

1 slice ginger root, minced

1 red pepper, cut into strips

1 green pepper, cut into strips

90 ml/6 tbsp chicken stock

Blanch the bean sprouts in boiling water for 3 minutes then drain. Heat the oil and fry the whole chilli peppers for about 3 minutes then discard the peppers. Add the ginger and peppers to the pan and stir-fry for 3 minutes. Add the bean sprouts and stir-fry for 2 minutes. Add the stock, bring to the boil, cover and simmer for 3 minutes before serving.

Bean Sprouts with Pork

Serves 4

450 g/1 lb bean sprouts

100 g/4 oz lean pork, cut into strips

15 ml/1 tbsp cornflour (cornstarch)

15 ml/1 tbsp rice wine

15 ml/1 tbsp soy sauce

5 ml/1 tsp sugar

2.5 ml/½ tsp salt

30 ml/2 tbsp groundnut (peanut) oil

75 ml/5 tbsp chicken stock

Blanch the bean sprouts in boiling water for 3 minutes then drain. Toss the pork with the cornflour, wine or sherry, soy sauce, sugar and salt then leave to stand for 30 minutes. Heat half the oil and stir-fry the bean sprouts for 1 minute. Remove from the pan. Heat the remaining oil and stir-fry the pork until lightly browned. Add the stock, cover and simmer for 3 minutes. Return the bean sprouts to the pan and stir until heated through. Serve at once.

Serves 4

45 ml/3 tbsp groundnut (peanut) oil

1 spring onion (scallion), chopped

450 g/1 lb broccoli florets

30 ml/2 tbsp soy sauce

5 ml/1 tsp sugar

120 ml/4 fl oz/½ cup chicken stock

5 ml/1 tsp cornflour (cornstarch)

Heat the oil and fry the spring onion until lightly browned. Add the broccoli and stir-fry for 3 minutes. Add the remaining ingredients and stir-fry for 2 minutes.

Broccoli in Brown Sauce

Serves 4

225 g/8 oz broccoli florets

30 ml/2 tbsp groundnut (peanut) oil

1 clove garlic, crushed

100 g/4 oz bamboo shoots, sliced

250 ml/8 fl oz/1 cup chicken stock

15 ml/1 tbsp soy sauce

15 ml/1 tbsp oyster sauce

15 ml/1 tbsp cornflour (cornstarch)

30 ml/2 tbsp rice wine or dry sherry

Parboil the broccoli in boiling water for 4 minutes then drain well. Heat the oil and fry the garlic until golden brown. Add the broccoli and bamboo shoots and stir-fry for 1 minute. Add the stock, soy sauce and oyster sauce, bring to the boil, cover and simmer for 4 minutes. Mix the cornflour and wine or sherry, stir it into the pan and simmer, stirring, until the sauce has thickened.

Serves 4

350 g/12 oz cabbage, finely shredded

salt

3 slices streaky bacon, rinded and cut into strips

30 ml/2 tbsp groundnut (peanut) oil

2 cloves garlic

5 ml/1 tsp grated ginger root

5 ml/1 tsp sugar

120 ml/4 fl oz/½ cup chicken or vegetable stock

Sprinkle the cabbage with salt and leave to stand for 15 minutes. Fry the bacon until crisp. Heat the oil and fry the garlic until lightly browned then discard. Add the cabbage to the pan with the ginger and sugar and stir-fry for 2 minutes. Add the stock and bacon and stir-fry for a further 2 minutes. Serve with fried rice.

Creamed Cabbage

Serves 4

450 g/1 lb Chinese cabbage

45 ml/3 tbsp groundnut (peanut) oil

250 ml/8 fl oz/1 cup chicken stock

salt

15 ml/1 tbsp cornflour (cornstarch)

50 g/2 oz smoked ham, diced

Cut the cabbage into 5 cm/2 in strips. Heat the oil and stir-fry the cabbage for 3 minutes. Add the stock and season with salt. Bring to the boil, cover and simmer for 4 minutes. Mix the cornflour with a little water, stir it into the pan and simmer, stirring, until the sauce thickens. Transfer to a warmed serving plate and serve sprinkled with ham.

Chinese Cabbage with Mushrooms

Serves 4

6 dried Chinese mushrooms

45 ml/3 tbsp groundnut (peanut) oil

1 Chinese cabbage, diced

1 red pepper, diced

1 green pepper, diced

225 g/8 oz garlic sausage, diced

120 ml/4 fl oz/½ cup chicken stock

45 ml/3 tbsp wine vinegar

20 ml/4 tsp soy sauce

20 ml/4 tsp honey

5 ml/1 tsp cornflour (cornstarch)

salt and freshly ground pepper

20 ml/2 tbsp chopped chives

Soak the mushrooms in warm water for 30 minutes then drain. Discard the stalks and chop the caps. Heat the oil and stir-fry the mushrooms, cabbage and peppers for 5 minutes. Add the garlic sausage and fry briefly. Mix the stock with the wine vinegar, soy sauce, honey and cornflour. Stir into the pan and bring to the boil. Season with salt and pepper and simmer, stirring, until the sauce thickens. Serve sprinkled with chives.

Spicy Cabbage Stir-Fry

Serves 4

450 g/1 lb cabbage, shredded

30 ml/2 tbsp groundnut (peanut) oil

2 cloves garlic, crushed

1 slice ginger root, minced

15 ml/1 tbsp oyster sauce

15 ml/1 tbsp soy sauce

15 ml/1 tbsp chilli bean sauce

5 ml/1 tsp sesame oil

Blanch the cabbage in boiling salted water for 2 minutes. Drain well. Heat the oil and stir-fry the garlic and ginger for a few seconds until lightly browned. Add the cabbage and stir-fry for 2 minutes. Add the remaining ingredients and stir-fry for a further 2 minutes.

Sweet and Sour Cabbage

Serves 4

15 ml/1 tbsp groundnut (peanut) oil

1 head cabbage, shredded

5 ml/1 tsp salt

30 ml/2 tbsp wine vinegar

30 ml/2 tbsp sugar

15 ml/1 tbsp soy sauce

15 ml/1 tbsp cornflour (cornstarch)

45 ml/3 tbsp water

Heat the oil and stir-fry the cabbage for 3 minutes. Add the salt and continue to stir-fry until the cabbage is just tender. Blend the wine vinegar, sugar, soy sauce, cornflour and water to a paste, add it to the pan and simmer, stirring, until the sauce coats the cabbage.

Sweet and Sour Red Cabbage

Serves 4

30 ml/2 tbsp groundnut (peanut) oil

450 g/1 lb red cabbage, shredded

50 g/2 oz/¼ cup brown sugar

45 ml/ 3 tbsp wine vinegar

15 ml/1 tbsp soy sauce

5 ml/ 1 tsp salt

15 ml/1 tbsp cornflour (cornstarch)

Heat the oil and stir-fry the cabbage for 4 minutes. Add the sugar, wine vinegar, soy sauce and salt and stir-fry for 2 minutes. Mix the cornflour with a little water and stir-fry for 1 minute.

Crispy Seaweed

Serves 4

750 g/1½ lb spring greens, very finely shredded
oil for deep-frying
5 ml/1 tsp salt
10 ml/2 tsp caster sugar

Rinse the greens then dry thoroughly. Heat the oil and deep-fry the greens in batches over a medium heat until they float to the surface. Remove from the oil and drain well on kitchen paper. Sprinkle with salt and sugar and toss together gently. Serve cold.

Carrots with Honey

Serves 4

1 kg/2 lb small spring carrots

20 ml/4 tsp groundnut (peanut) oil

20 ml/4 tsp unsalted butter

15 ml/1 tbsp water

10 ml/2 tsp honey

15 ml/1 tbsp chopped fresh coriander

100 g/4 oz pine kernels

salt and freshly ground pepper

Wash the carrots and cut the green down to 5 mm/¼ in. Heat the oil and butter, add the water and honey and bring to the boil. Add the carrots and cook for about 4 minutes. Add the coriander and pine kernels and season with salt and pepper.

Serves 4

30 ml/2 tbsp groundnut (peanut) oil

2.5 ml/½ tsp salt

4 carrots, sliced

1 green pepper, cut into strips

30 ml/2 tbsp sugar

15 ml/1 tbsp wine vinegar

250 ml/8 fl oz/1 cup chicken tock

15 ml/1 tbsp cornflour (cornstarch)

Heat the oil and salt then add the carrots and pepper and stir-fry for 3 minutes. Add the sugar, wine vinegar and half the stock, bring to the boil, cover and simmer for 5 minutes. Stir the cornflour into the remaining stock, add to the pan and simmer, stirring, until the sauce thickens and clears.

Stir-Fried Cauliflower

Serves 4

450 g/1 lb cauliflower florets

45 ml/3 tbsp groundnut (peanut) oil

1 spring onion (scallion), chopped

120 ml/4 fl oz/½ cup chicken stock

5 ml/1 tsp cornflour (cornstarch)

Blanch the cauliflower in boiling water for 2 minutes then drain well. Heat the oil and fry the spring onion until lightly browned. Add the cauliflower and stir-fry for 4 minutes. Add the remaining ingredients and stir-fry for 2 minutes.

Serves 4

6 dried Chinese mushrooms

1 small cauliflower

45 ml/3 tbsp groundnut (peanut) oil

100 g/4 oz water chestnuts, sliced

45 ml/3 tbsp soy sauce

15 ml/1 tbsp rice wine or dry sherry

5 ml/1 tsp cornflour (cornstarch)

30 ml/2 tbsp water

Soak the mushrooms in warm water for 30 minutes then drain, reserving 120 ml/4 fl oz/½ cup of liquid. Discard the stalks and slice the caps. Cut the cauliflower into small florets. Heat the oil and stir-fry the mushrooms until coated with oil. Add the water chestnuts and stir-fry for 1 minute. Mix the soy sauce and wine or sherry with the mushroom liquid and add it to the pan with the cauliflower. Bring to the boil, cover and simmer for 5 minutes. Blend the cornflour and water to a paste, stir into the sauce and simmer, stirring, until the sauce thickens.

Serves 4

30 ml/2 tbsp groundnut (peanut) oil

6 spring onions (scallions), chopped

½ head celery, cut into chunks

15 ml/1 tbsp soy sauce

5 ml/1 tsp salt

Heat the oil and fry the spring onions until lightly browned. Add the celery and stir until well coated with oil. Add the soy sauce and salt, stir well, cover and simmer for 3 minutes.

Serves 4

45 ml/3 tbsp groundnut (peanut) oil
6 stalks celery, diagonally sliced
225 g/8 oz mushrooms, sliced
30 ml/2 tbsp rice wine or dry sherry
salt and freshly ground pepper

Heat the oil and stir-fry the celery for 3 minutes. Add the mushrooms and stir-fry for 2 minutes. Add the wine or sherry and season with salt and pepper. Stir-fry for a few minutes until heated through.

Stir-Fried Chinese Leaves

Serves 4

15 ml/1 tbsp groundnut (peanut) oil

1 clove garlic, chopped

3 spring onions (scallions), chopped

350 g/12 oz Chinese leaves, shredded

2.5 ml/½ tsp salt

450 ml/¾ pt boiling water

Heat the oil and fry the garlic and onion until lightly browned. Add the Chinese leaves and salt and stir well. Add the boiling water, return to the boil, cover arid simmer for about 5 minutes until the Chinese leaves are tender but still crisp. Drain well.

Chinese Leaves in Milk

Serves 4

350 g/12 oz Chinese leaves, shredded

45 ml/3 tbsp groundnut (peanut) oil

3 spring onions (scallions), chopped

15 ml/1 tbsp rice wine or dry sherry

90 ml/6 tbsp chicken stock

salt

90 ml/6 tbsp milk

15 ml/1 tbsp cornflour (cornstarch)

5 ml/1 tsp sesame oil

Steam the Chinese leaves for about 5 minutes until just tender. Heat the oil and fry the spring onions until lightly browned. Add the wine or sherry and chicken stock and season with salt. Stir in the cabbage, cover and simmer gently for 5 minutes. Mix the milk and cornflour, stir into pan and simmer, stirring, for 2 minutes. Serve sprinkled with sesame oil.

Serves 4

50 g/2 oz dried Chinese mushrooms

450 g/1 lb Chinese leaves

45 ml/3 tbsp groundnut (peanut) oil

120 ml/4 fl oz/½ cup chicken stock

15 ml/1 tbsp soy sauce

5 ml/1 tsp salt

5 ml/1 tsp sugar

15 ml/1 tbsp cornflour (cornstarch)

10 ml/2 tsp sesame oil

Soak the mushrooms in warm water for 30 minutes then drain. Discard the stems and slice the caps. Cut the head of Chinese leaves into thick slices. Heat half the oil, add the Chinese leaves and stir-fry for 2 minutes. Add the chicken stock, soy sauce, salt and sugar and stir-fry for about 4 minutes. Add the mushrooms and stir-fry until the vegetables are tender. Mix the cornflour with a little water, stir it into the sauce and simmer, stirring until the sauce clears and thickens. Serve sprinkled with sesame oil.

Serves 4

4 hearts Chinese leaves
600 ml/1 pt/2½ cups chicken stock
100 g/4 oz shelled scallops, sliced
5 ml/1 tsp cornflour (cornstarch)

Place the Chinese leaves and stock in a pan, bring to the boil and simmer for about 10 minutes until just tender. Transfer the Chinese leaves to a warmed serving plate and keep them warm. Pour out all but 250 ml/8 fl oz/1 cup of the stock. Add the scallops and simmer for a few minutes until the scallops are tender. Blend the cornflour with a little water, stir it into the pan and simmer, stirring, until the sauce thickens slightly. Pour over the Chinese leaves and serve.

Steamed Chinese Leaves

Serves 4

450 g/1 lb Chinese leaves, separated

15 ml/1 tbsp cornflour (cornstarch)

5 ml/1 tsp salt

300 ml/½ pt/1¼ cups chicken stock

Arrange the leaves in an ovenproof bowl, place it on a rack in a steamer and steam over gently boiling water for 15 minutes. Meanwhile, blend the cornflour, salt and stock over a gentle heat, bring to the boil and simmer, stirring, until the mixture thickens. Arrange the Chinese leaves on a warmed serving plate, pour over the sauce and serve.

Serves 4

450 g/1 lb Chinese leaves, shredded

45 ml/3 tbsp groundnut (peanut) oil

100 g/4 oz water chestnuts, sliced

250 ml/8 fl oz/1 cup chicken stock

15 ml/1 tbsp soy sauce

15 ml/1 tbsp cornflour (cornstarch)

15 ml/1 tbsp water

Blanch the Chinese leaves in boiling water for 2 minutes then drain. Heat the oil and stir-fry the water chestnuts for 2 minutes. Add the Chinese leaves and stir-fry for 3 minutes. Add the chicken stock and soy sauce, bring to the boil, cover and simmer for 5 minutes. Mix the cornflour and water to a paste, stir into the pan and simmer, stirring, until the sauce clears and thickens.

Serves 4

45 ml/3 tbsp groundnut (peanut) oil

1 spring onion (scallion), chopped

450 g/1 lb courgettes (zucchini), thickly sliced

30 ml/2 tbsp soy sauce

5 ml/1 tsp sugar

120 ml/4 fl oz/½ cup chicken stock

5 ml/1 tsp cornflour (cornstarch)

Heat the oil and fry the spring onion until lightly browned. Add the courgettes and stir-fry for 3 minutes. Add the remaining ingredients and stir-fry for 4 minutes.

Serves 4

30 ml/2 tbsp groundnut (peanut) oil

1 clove garlic, crushed

5 ml/1 tsp salt

15 ml/1 tbsp chilli bean sauce

450 g/1 lb courgettes (zucchini), thickly sliced

30 ml/2 tbsp rice wine or dry sherry

45 ml/3 tbsp water

15 ml/1 tbsp sesame oil

Heat the oil and fry the garlic, salt and chilli bean sauce for a few seconds. Add the courgettes and stir-fry for 3 minutes until lightly browned. Add the remaining ingredients, including sesame oil to taste, and stir-fry for 1 minute.

Stuffed Courgette Bites

Serves 4

4 large courgettes (zucchini)
225 g/8 oz minced (ground) pork
225 g/8 oz crab meat, flaked
2 eggs, beaten
30 ml/2 tbsp soy sauce
30 ml/2 tbsp oyster sauce
pinch of ground ginger
salt and freshly ground pepper
75 ml/5 tbsp cornflour (cornstarch)
50 g/2 oz/½ cup breadcrumbs
oil for deep-frying

Cut the courgettes in half lengthways and remove the seeds and cores with a spoon. Mix the pork, crab meat, eggs, sauces, ginger, salt and pepper. Bind with the cornflour and breadcrumbs. Cover and chill for 30 minutes. Fill the courgettes with the mixture then cut them into chunks. Heat the oil and deep-fry the courgettes until golden. Drain on kitchen paper before serving.

Cucumber with Prawns

Serves 4

45 ml/3 tbsp groundnut (peanut) oil

100 g/4 oz peeled prawns

1 cucumber, peeled and thickly sliced

30 ml/2 tbsp soy sauce

5 ml/1 tsp rice wine or dry sherry

5 ml/1 tsp brown sugar

salt

45 ml/3 tbsp water

Heat the oil and stir-fry the prawns for 30 seconds. Add the cucumber and stir-fry for 1 minute. Add the soy sauce, wine or sherry and sugar and season with salt. Stir-fry for 3 minutes, adding a little water if necessary. Serve immediately.

Serves 4

1 large cucumber

salt

30 ml/2 tbsp sesame oil

2.5 ml/½ tsp sugar

Peel the cucumber and cut in half lengthways. Scoop out the seeds then cut into thick slices. Arrange the cucumber slices in a colander and sprinkle generously with salt. Leave to stand for 1 hour then press out as much moisture as possible. Heat the oil and stir-fry the cucumbers for 2 minutes until softened. Stir in the sugar and serve at once.

Stuffed Cucumbers

Serves 4

225 g/8 oz minced (ground) pork

1 egg, beaten

30 ml/2 tbsp cornflour (cornstarch)

15 ml/1 tbsp rice wine or dry sherry

30 ml/2 tbsp soy sauce

salt and freshly ground pepper

2 large cucumbers

30 ml/2 tbsp plain (all-purpose) flour

45 ml/3 tbsp groundnut (peanut) oil

150 ml/¼ pt/generous ½ cup chicken stock

30 ml/2 tbsp water

Mix together the pork, egg, half the cornflour, the wine or sherry and half the soy sauce and season with salt and pepper. Peel the cucumbers then cut into 5 cm/2 in chunks. Scoop out some of the seeds to make hollows and fill with stuffing, pressing it down. Dust with flour. Heat the oil and fry the cucumber pieces, stuffing side down, until lightly browned. Turn over and cook until the other side is browned. Add the stock and soy sauce, bring to the boil, cover and simmer for 20 minutes until tender, turning occasionally. Transfer the cucumbers to a warmed serving plate. Mix the remaining cornflour with the water, stir it into the pan and simmer, stirring, until the sauce clears and thickens. Pour over the cucumbers and serve.

Stir-Fried Dandelion Leaves

Serves 4

30 ml/2 tbsp groundnut (peanut) oil
450 g/1 lb dandelion leaves
5 ml/1 tsp salt
15 ml/1 tbsp sugar

Heat the oil, add the dandelion leaves, salt and sugar and stir-fry over a moderate heat for 5 minutes. Serve at once.

Serves 4

1 head crisp lettuce

15 ml/1 tbsp groundnut (peanut) oil

2.5 ml/½ tsp salt

1 clove garlic, crushed

60 ml/4 tbsp chicken stock

5 ml/1 tsp soy sauce

Separate the lettuce into leaves. Heat the oil and fry the salt and garlic until lightly browned. Add the lettuce and simmer for 1 minute, stirring to coat the lettuce in oil. Add the stock and simmer for 2 minutes. Serve sprinkled with soy sauce.

Stir-Fried Lettuce with Ginger

Serves 4

45 ml/3 tbsp groundnut (peanut) oil

2 cloves garlic, crushed

1 cm/½ in slice ginger root, finely chopped

1 head lettuce, shredded

Heat the oil and fry the garlic and ginger until light golden. Add the lettuce and stir-fry for about 2 minutes until glossy and slightly wilted. Serve at once.

Mangetout with Bamboo Shoots

Serves 4

30 ml/2 tbsp groundnut (peanut) oil

100 g/4 oz minced (ground) pork

100 g/4 oz mushrooms

225 g/8 oz bamboo shoots, sliced

225 g/8 oz mangetout (snow peas)

15 ml/1 tbsp soy sauce

15 ml/1 tbsp cornflour (cornstarch)

5 ml/1 tsp sugar

120 ml/4 fl oz/½ cup chicken stock

Heat the oil and fry the pork until lightly browned. Stir in the mushrooms and bamboo shoots and stir-fry for 2 minutes. Add the mangetout and stir-fry for 2 minutes. Sprinkle with soy sauce. Mix the cornflour, sugar and stock to a paste, stir into the pan and simmer, stirring, until the sauce thickens.

Mangetout with Mushrooms and Ginger

Serves 4

45 ml/3 tbsp groundnut (peanut) oil

3 spring onions (scallions), sliced

1 slice ginger root, minced

225 g/8 oz mushrooms, halved

300 ml/½ pt/1¼ cup chicken stock

10 ml/2 tsp cornflour (cornstarch)

15 ml/1 tbsp water

15 ml/1 tbsp oyster sauce

225 g/8 oz mangetout (snow peas)

Heat the oil and fry the spring onions and ginger until lightly browned. Add the mushrooms and stir-fry for 3 minutes. Add the stock, bring to the boil, cover and simmer for 3 minutes. Blend the cornflour to a paste with the water and oyster sauce, stir it into the pan and simmer, stirring, until the sauce thickens. Stir in the mangetout and heat through before serving.

Serves 4

60 ml/4 tbsp groundnut (peanut) oil
450 g/1 lb marrow, thinly sliced
30 ml/2 tbsp soy sauce
10 ml/2 tsp salt
freshly ground pepper

Heat the oil and stir-fry the marrow slices for 2 minutes. Add the soy sauce, salt and a pinch of pepper and stir-fry for a further 4 minutes.

Stuffed Marrow

Serves 4

450 g/1 lb fish fillets, flaked

5 ml/1 tsp salt

2 spring onions (scallions), chopped

100 g/4 oz smoked ham, chopped

50 g/2 oz/½ cup chopped almonds

1 marrow, halved

oil for deep-frying

250 ml/8 fl oz/1 cup chicken stock

30 ml/2 tbsp cornflour (cornstarch)

15 ml/1 tbsp soy sauce

5 ml/1 tsp sugar

60 ml/4 tbsp water

5 ml/1 tsp sesame oil

15 ml/1 tbsp chopped flat-leaved parsley

Mix the fish, salt, spring onions, ham and almonds. Scoop out the seeds of the marrow and some of the flesh to make a hollow. Press the fish mixture into the marrow. Heat the oil and deep-fry the marrow halves, one at a time if necessary, until golden brown. Transfer to a clean pan and add the stock. Bring to the boil, cover and simmer for 40 minutes. Blend the cornflour, soy sauce, sugar, water and sesame oil to a paste, stir into the pan and simmer, stirring, until the sauce clears and thickens. Serve garnished with parsley.

Mushrooms with Anchovy Sauce

Serves 4

15 ml/1 tbsp groundnut (peanut) oil
450 g/1 lb button mushrooms
2 shallots, sliced
1 stick lemon grass, chopped
1 large tomato, diced
60 ml/4 tbsp chopped flat-leaved parsley
20 ml/4 tsp anchovy paste
50 g/2 oz/½ cup butter
salt and freshly ground pepper
4 slices bread
8 anchovy fillets

Heat the oil and fry the mushrooms, shallots and lemon grass until lightly browned. Add the tomato and half the parsley and stir well. Mix in the anchovy paste and the butter, cut into flakes. Season with salt and pepper. Toast the bread then sprinkle with the remaining parsley. Arrange the anchovy fillets on top and serve with the mushrooms.

Serves 4

45 ml/3 tbsp groundnut (peanut) oil

5 ml/1 tsp salt

1 clove garlic, crushed

225 g/8 oz bamboo shoots, sliced

225 g/8 oz mushrooms, sliced

45 ml/3 tbsp soy sauce

15 ml/1 tbsp rice wine or dry sherry

15 ml/1 tbsp sugar

15 ml/1 tbsp cornflour (cornstarch)

90 ml/6 tbsp chicken stock

Heat the oil and fry the salt and garlic until the garlic turns light golden. Add the bamboo shoots and mushrooms and stir-fry for 3 minutes. Add the soy sauce, wine or sherry and sugar and stir-fry for 3 minutes. Mix the cornflour and stock and stir it into the pan. Bring to the boil, stirring, then simmer for a few minutes until the sauce thickens and clears.

Serves 4

8 dried Chinese mushrooms

30 ml/2 tbsp groundnut (peanut) oil

100 g/4 oz mangetout (snow peas)

100 g/4 oz bamboo shoots, sliced

60 ml/4 tbsp stock

30 ml/2 tbsp soy sauce

5 ml/1 tsp sugar

Soak the mushrooms in warm water for 30 minutes then drain. Discard the stalks and slice the caps. Heat the oil and fry the mangetout for about 30 seconds then remove from the pan. Add the mushrooms and bamboo shoots and stir-fry until well coated with oil. Add the stock, soy sauce and sugar, bring to the boil, cover and simmer gently for 3 minutes. Return the mangetout to the pan and simmer, uncovered, until heated through. Serve at once.

Serves 4

30 ml/2 tbsp groundnut (peanut) oil
225 g/8 oz button mushrooms
450 g/1 lb mangetout (snow peas)
15 ml/1 tbsp soy sauce
10 ml/2 tsp sesame oil
5 ml/1 tsp brown sugar

Heat the oil and fry the mushrooms for 5 minutes. Add the mangetout and stir-fry for 1 minute. Add the remaining ingredients and stir-fry for 4 minutes.

Serves 4

15 ml/1 tbsp groundnut (peanut) oil

1 clove garlic, finely chopped

1 slice ginger root, minced

2 spring onions (scallions), chopped

225 g/8 oz button mushrooms

15 ml/1 tbsp hoisin sauce

15 ml/1 tbsp rice wine or dry sherry

45 ml/3 tbsp chicken stock

5 ml/1 tsp sesame oil

Heat the oil and stir-fry the garlic, ginger and spring onions for 2 minutes. Add the mushrooms and stir-fry for 2 minutes. Add the remaining ingredients and stir-fry for 5 minutes.

Steamed Mushrooms

Serves 4

18 dried Chinese mushrooms

450 ml/¾ pt/2 cups stock

30 ml/2 tbsp groundnut (peanut) oil

5 ml/1 tsp sugar

Soak the mushrooms in warm water for 30 minutes then drain, reserving 250 ml/8 fl oz/1 cup of soaking liquid. Discard the stalks and arrange the caps in a heatproof bowl. Add the remaining ingredients, stand the bowl on a rack in a steamer, cover and steam over boiling water for about 1 hour.

Steamed Stuffed Mushrooms

Serves 4

450 g/1 lb large mushrooms

225 g/8 oz minced (ground) pork

225 g/8 oz peeled prawns, finely chopped

4 water chestnuts, finely chopped

15 ml/1 tbsp cornflour (cornstarch)

5 ml/1 tsp salt

5 ml/1 tsp sugar

30 ml/2 tbsp soy sauce

120 ml/4 fl oz/½ cup

Remove the stalks from the mushrooms. Chop the stalks and mix them with the remaining ingredients. Arrange the mushroom caps on an ovenproof plate and top with the stuffing mixture, pressing it down into a dome shape. Spoon a little stock over each one, reserving a little stock. Place the plate on a rack in a steamer, cover and steam over gently simmering water for about 45 minutes until the mushrooms are cooked, basting with a little more stock during cooking if necessary.

Straw Mushrooms in Oyster Sauce

Serves 4

15 ml/1 tbsp groundnut (peanut) oil

225 g/8 oz straw mushrooms

120 ml/4 fl oz/½ cup chicken stock

2.5 ml/½ tsp sugar

5 ml/1 tsp oyster sauce

5 ml/1 tsp cornflour (cornstarch)

15 ml/1 tbsp water

Heat the oil and fry the mushrooms gently until well coated. Add the stock, sugar and oyster sauce, bring to the boil then simmer gently until the mushrooms are tender. Mix the cornflour and water to a paste, stir into the pan and simmer, stirring, until the sauce clears and thickens.

Serves 4

8 large onions

salt and freshly ground pepper

30 ml/2 tbsp groundnut (peanut) oil

120 ml/4 fl oz/½ cup water

15 ml/1 tbsp cornflour (cornstarch)

15 ml/1 tbsp chopped fresh parsley

Put the onions in a pan and just cover with boiling salted water. Cover and simmer for 5 minutes then drain. Arrange the onions in an ovenproof dish, season with salt and pepper and brush with oil. Pour in the water, cover and bake in a preheated oven at 190°C/375°F/gas mark 5 for 1 hour. Blend the cornflour with a little water and stir it into the onion liquid. Bake for a further 5 minutes, stirring occasionally, until the sauce thickens. Serve garnished with parsley.

Curried Onions with Peas

Serves 4

450 g/1 lb pearl onions

10 ml/2 tsp salt

225 g/8 oz peas

45 ml/3 tbsp groundnut (peanut) oil

10 ml/2 tsp curry powder

freshly ground pepper

Place the onions in a pan and just cover with boiling water. Season with 5 ml/1 tsp of salt and boil for 5 minutes. Cover and boil for a further 10 minutes. Add the peas and cook for a further 5 minutes then drain. Heat the oil and fry the curry powder, remaining salt and remaining pepper for 30 seconds. Add the drained vegetables and stir-fry until hot and glazed with the curry oil.

Pearl Onions in Orange-Ginger Sauce

Serves 4

3 oranges

2 red chilli peppers

15 ml/1 tbsp walnut oil

450 g/1 lb pearl onions

1 slice ginger root, chopped

10 ml/2 tsp sugar

10 ml/2 tsp cider vinegar

15 ml/1 tbsp red peppercorns

salt

5 ml/1 tsp grated lemon rind

a few coriander leaves

Using a zester, cut the orange peel into narrow slivers. Halve the oranges and squeeze the juice. Halve the chilli peppers and remove the seeds. Heat the oil and stir-fry the onions, ginger and chilli peppers for 1 minute. Add the sugar then simmer until the onions are translucent. Mix in the orange juice, cider vinegar, peppercorns and orange rind and season with salt. Stir in the lemon rind and most of the coriander leaves. Arrange on a warmed serving plate and garnish with the remaining coriander leaves.

Onion Custard

Serves 4

4 rashers bacon

450 g/1 lb onions, sliced

50 g/2 oz/½ cup cornflour (cornstarch)

2 eggs, lightly beaten

120 ml/4 fl oz/½ cup water

pinch of grated nutmeg

10 ml/2 tsp salt

Fry the bacon until crisp then drain and chop. Add the onions to the pan and fry until softened. Beat the cornflour with the eggs and water and season with nutmeg and salt. Mix the bacon with the onions and place in a greased ovenproof dish. Top with the egg mixture and stand the dish in a roasting tin half filled with water. Bake in a preheated oven at 180°C/ 350°F/gas mark 4 for 45 minutes until the custard is set.

Serves 4

45 ml/3 tbsp groundnut (peanut) oil

2 spring onions (scallions), chopped

450 g/1 lb pak choi, shredded

15 ml/1 tbsp soy sauce

2.5 ml/½ tsp sugar

120 ml/4 fl oz/½ cup chicken stock

5 ml/1 tsp cornflour (cornstarch)

Heat the oil and fry the spring onions until lightly browned. Add the pak choi and stir-fry for 3 minutes. Add the remaining ingredients and stir-fry for 2 minutes.

Peas with Mushrooms

Serves 4

45 ml/3 tbsp groundnut (peanut) oil

1 spring onion (scallion), chopped

225 g/8 oz mushrooms, halved

225 g/8 oz frozen peas

30 ml/2 tbsp soy sauce

5 ml/1 tsp sugar

120 ml/4 fl oz/½ cup chicken stock

5 ml/1 tsp cornflour (cornstarch)

Heat the oil and fry the spring onion until lightly browned. Add the mushrooms and stir-fry for 3 minutes. Add the peas and stir-fry for 4 minutes. Add the remaining ingredients and stir-fry for 2 minutes.

Stir-Fried Peppers

Serves 4

30 ml/2 tbsp groundnut (peanut) oil

2 green peppers, cubed

2 red peppers, cubed

15 ml/1 tbsp chicken stock or water

5 ml/1 tsp salt

5 ml/1 tsp brown sugar

Heat the oil until very hot, add the peppers and stir-fry until the skins wrinkle slightly. Add the stock or water, salt and sugar and stir-fry for 2 minutes.

Pepper and Bean Stir-Fry

Serves 4

30 ml/2 tbsp groundnut (peanut) oil

2 cloves garlic, crushed

5 ml/1 tsp salt

2 red peppers, cut into strips

225 g/8 oz French beans

5 ml/1 tsp sugar

30 ml/2 tbsp water

Heat the oil and stir-fry the garlic, salt, peppers and beans for 3 minutes. Add the sugar and water and stir-fry for about 5 minutes until the vegetables are tender but still crisp.

Fish-Stuffed Peppers

Serves 4

225 g/8 oz fish fillets, flaked

2 spring onions (scallions), minced

30 ml/2 tbsp cornflour (cornstarch)

15 ml/1 tbsp groundnut (peanut) oil

30 ml/2 tbsp water

salt and freshly ground pepper

4 green peppers

120 ml/4 fl oz/½ cup chicken stock

2.5 ml/½ tsp salt

60 ml/4 tbsp water

Mix together the fish, spring onions, half the cornflour, the oil and water and season with salt and pepper. Cut the tops off the peppers and scoop out the seeds. Fill with the stuffing mixture and replace the tops as lids. Stand the peppers upright in a pan and add the stock. Bring to the boil and season with salt and pepper. Cover and simmer for 1 hour. Transfer the peppers to a warmed serving dish. Blend the remaining cornflour and water to a paste, stir into the pan and bring to the boil. Simmer, stirring, until the sauce clears and thickens. Pour over the peppers and serve at once.

Pork-Stuffed Peppers

Serves 4

30 ml/2 tbsp groundnut (peanut) oil

225 g/8 oz minced (ground) pork

2 spring onions (scallions), chopped

4 water chestnuts, chopped

30 ml/2 tbsp soy sauce

salt and freshly ground pepper

4 green peppers

120 ml/4 fl oz/½ cup chicken stock

2.5 ml/½ tsp salt

15 ml/1 tbsp cornflour (cornstarch)

60 ml/4 tbsp water

Heat the oil and fry the pork, spring onions and water chestnuts until lightly browned. Remove from the heat, stir half the soy sauce and season with salt and pepper. Cut the tops off the peppers and scoop out the seeds. Fill with the stuffing mixture and replace the tops as lids. Stand the peppers upright in a pan and add the stock. Bring to the boil and season with salt and pepper. Cover and simmer for 1 hour. Transfer the peppers to a warmed serving dish. Blend the cornflour, remaining soy sauce and water to a paste, stir into the pan and bring to the boil.

Simmer, stirring, until the sauce clears and thickens. Pour over the peppers and serve at once.

Vegetable-Stuffed Peppers

Serves 4

30 ml/2 tbsp groundnut (peanut) oil

2 carrots, grated

1 onion, grated

45 ml/3 tbsp tomato ketchup (catsup)

5 ml/1 tsp sugar

salt and freshly ground pepper

4 green peppers

120 ml/4 fl oz/½ cup chicken stock

2.5 ml/½ tsp salt

15 ml/1 tbsp cornflour (cornstarch)

15 ml/1 tbsp soy sauce

60 ml/4 tbsp water

Heat the oil and fry the carrots and onions until slightly softened. Remove from the heat and stir in the tomato ketchup and sugar. Season with salt and pepper. Cut the tops off the peppers and scoop out the seeds. Fill with the stuffing mixture and replace the tops as lids. Stand the peppers upright in a pan and add the stock. Bring to the boil and season with salt and pepper. Cover and simmer for 1 hour. Transfer the peppers to a warmed serving dish. Blend the cornflour, soy sauce and water to a paste, stir into the pan and bring to the boil. Simmer, stirring, until the sauce clears and thickens. Pour over the peppers and serve at once.

Deep-Fried Potatoes and Carrots

Serves 4

2 carrots, diced
450 g/1 lb potatoes
15 ml/1 tbsp cornflour (cornstarch)
oil for deep-frying
30 ml/2 tbsp groundnut (peanut) oil
5 ml/1 tsp salt
15 ml/1 tbsp rice wine or dry sherry
120 ml/4 fl oz/½ cup chicken stock
5 ml/1 tsp sugar
5 ml/1 tsp soy sauce

Blanch the carrots in boiling water for 3 minutes then drain. Cut the potatoes into chips and dust with a little cornflour. Heat the oil and deep-fry until crisp then drain. Heat the oil and salt and stir-fry the carrots until coated with oil. Add the wine or sherry and stock, bring to the boil, cover and simmer for 2 minutes. Blend the remaining cornflour to a paste with the sugar and soy sauce. Stir into the pan and simmer, stirring, until the sauce thickens. Add the potatoes and reheat. Serve at once.

Potato Sauté

Serves 4

350 g/12 oz potatoes, peeled and cut into matchsticks

30 ml/2 tbsp groundnut (peanut) oil

1 clove garlic, crushed

3 spring onions (scallions), chopped

15 ml/1 tbsp soy sauce

5 ml/1 tsp wine vinegar

salt and freshly ground pepper

Blanch the potatoes in boiling water for 20 seconds then drain. Heat the oil and fry the garlic and spring onions until lightly browned. Add the potatoes and stir-fry for 2 minutes. Add the soy sauce and wine vinegar and season to taste with salt and pepper. Fry for a few minutes until the potatoes are cooked and lightly browned.

Spiced Potatoes

Serves 4

30 ml/2 tbsp groundnut (peanut) oil
350 g/12 oz potatoes, peeled and diced
1 clove garlic, crushed
2.5 ml/½ tsp salt
2 spring onions (scallions), chopped
2 dried chilli peppers, seeded and chopped

Heat the oil and fry the potatoes until lightly golden. Remove them from the pan. Reheat the oil and fry the garlic, salt, spring onions and chilli peppers until lightly browned. Return the potatoes to the pan and stir-fry until the potatoes are cooked.

Pumpkin with Rice Noodles

Serves 4

350 g/12 oz rice noodles

15 ml/1 tbsp groundnut (peanut) oil

2 spring onions (scallions), sliced

225 g/8 oz pumpkin, cubed

250 ml/8 fl oz/1 cup chicken stock

2.5 ml/½ tsp sugar

salt and freshly ground pepper

100 g/4 oz peeled prawns

Blanch the noodles in boiling water for 2 minutes then drain. Heat the oil and stir-fry the spring onions for 30 seconds. Add the pumpkin and stir-fry for 1 minute. Add the stock and noodles, bring to the boil and simmer, uncovered, for about 5 minutes until the pumpkin is almost cooked. Add the sugar and season with salt and pepper. Simmer for about 10 minutes until the noodles are just tender and the liquid has reduced slightly. Add the prawns and heat through before serving.

Shallots in Malt Beer

Serves 4

15 ml/1 tbsp walnut oil

450 g/1 lb shallots

10 ml/2 tsp brown sugar

5 ml/1 tsp red peppercorns

250 ml/8 fl oz/1 cup malt beer

45 ml/3 tbsp balsamic vinegar

salt and freshly ground pepper

2.5 ml/½ tsp paprika

1 lamb's lettuce

Heat the oil and fry the shallots until golden brown. Add the sugar and stir-fry until translucent. Add the peppercorns, beer and balsamic vinegar and simmer for 1 minute. Season with salt, pepper and paprika. Arrange the lettuce leaves around the edge of a warmed serving plate and spoon the shallots into the centre.

Spinach with Garlic

Serves 4

30 ml/2 tbsp groundnut (peanut) oil

450 g/1 lb spinach leaves

2.5 ml/½ tsp salt

3 cloves garlic, crushed

15 ml/1 tbsp soy sauce

Heat the oil, add the spinach and salt and stir-fry for 3 minutes until the spinach begins to wilt. Add the garlic and soy sauce and stir-fry for 3 minutes before serving.

Spinach with Mushrooms

Serves 4–6

8 dried Chinese mushrooms

75 ml/5 tbsp groundnut (peanut) oil

60 ml/4 tbsp soy sauce

15 ml/1 tbsp rice wine or dry sherry

5 ml/1 tsp sugar

salt

15 ml/1 tbsp cornflour (cornstarch)

15 ml/1 tbsp water

450 g/1 lb spinach

Soak the mushrooms in warm water for 30 minutes then drain, reserving 120 ml/4 fl oz/½ cup of soaking liquid. Discard the stalks and cut the caps in half, if large. Heat half the oil and fry the mushrooms for 2 minutes. Stir in the soy sauce, wine or sherry, sugar and a pinch of salt and mix well. Add the mushroom liquid, bring to the boil, cover and simmer for 10 minutes. Blend the cornflour and water to a paste, stir it into the sauce and simmer, stirring, until the sauce thickens. Leave over a very low heat to keep warm. Meanwhile, heat the remaining oil in a separate pan, add the spinach and stir-fry for about 2 minutes until softened. Transfer to a warmed serving dish, pour over the mushrooms and serve.

Spinach with Ginger

Serves 4

30 ml/2 tbsp groundnut (peanut) oil
1 slice ginger root, minced
1 clove garlic, crushed
5 ml/1 tsp salt
450 g/1 lb spinach
5 ml/1 tsp sugar
10 ml/2 tsp sesame oil

Heat the oil and stir-fry the ginger, garlic and salt until lightly browned. Add the spinach and stir-fry for 3 minutes until wilted. Add the sugar and sesame oil and stir-fry for 3 minutes. Serve hot or cold.

Serves 4

30 ml/2 tbsp peanuts

450 g/1 lb spinach, shredded

2.5 ml/½ tsp salt

100 g/4 oz smoked ham, chopped

15 ml/1 tbsp groundnut (peanut) oil

Toast the peanuts in a dry pan then chop coarsely. Blanch the spinach in boiling water for 2 minutes then drain well and chop. Mix in the peanuts, salt, ham and oil and serve at once.

Vegetable Chow Mein

Serves 4

6 dried Chinese mushrooms
450 g/1 lb spinach
45 ml/3 tbsp groundnut (peanut) oil
100 g/4 oz bamboo shoots, sliced
2.5 ml/½ tsp salt
30 ml/2 tbsp soy sauce
soft-fried noodles

Soak the mushrooms in warm water for 30 minutes then drain. Discard the stalks and slice the caps. Halve the spinach leaves. Heat the oil and stir-fry the mushrooms and bamboo shoots for 4 minutes. Add the spinach, salt and soy sauce and stir-fry for 1 minute. Add the drained noodles and stir gently until heated through.

Mixed Vegetables

Serves 4

2 onions

30 ml/2 tbsp groundnut (peanut) oil

15 ml/1 tbsp grated ginger root

225 g/8 oz broccoli florets

225 g/8 oz spinach, chopped

225 g/8 oz mangetout (snow peas)

4 stalks celery, diagonally sliced

6 spring onions (scallions), diagonally sliced

175 ml/6 fl oz/¾ cup vegetable stock

Cut the onions into wedges and separate the layers. Heat the oil and stir-fry the onions, ginger and broccoli for 1 minute. Add the remaining vegetables and toss lightly. Add the stock and toss until the vegetables are completely coated. Bring to the boil, cover and simmer for 3 minutes until the vegetables are tender but still crisp.

Mixed Vegetables with Ginger

Serves 4

100 g/4 oz cauliflower florets

45 ml/3 tbsp groundnut (peanut) oil

2 slices ginger root, minced

1 spring onion (scallion), chopped

100 g/4 oz bamboo shoots, sliced

100 g/4 oz mushrooms, sliced

100 g/4 oz Chinese cabbage, shredded

30 ml/2 tbsp soy sauce

120 ml/4 fl oz/½ cup chicken stock

salt and freshly ground pepper

Blanch the cauliflower in boiling water for 3 minutes then drain. Heat the oil and stir-fry the ginger for 1 minute. Add the vegetables and stir-fry for 3 minutes until coated with oil. Add the soy sauce and stock and season with salt and pepper. Stir-fry for a further 2 minutes until the vegetables are just tender but still crisp.

Vegetable Spring Rolls

Serves 4

6 dried Chinese mushrooms

30 ml/2 tbsp groundnut (peanut) oil

2.5 ml/½ tsp salt

2 cloves garlic, finely chopped

2 stalks celery, chopped

1 green pepper, sliced

50 g/2 oz bamboo shoots, sliced

100 g/4 oz Chinese leaves, shredded

100 g/4 oz bean sprouts

4 water chestnuts, cut into strips

3 spring onions (scallions), chopped

15 ml/1 tbsp soy sauce

5 ml/1 tsp sugar

8 spring roll skins

groundnut (peanut) oil for frying

Soak the mushrooms in warm water for 30 minutes then drain. Discard the stems and chop the caps. Heat the oil, salt and garlic until the garlic turns golden then add the mushrooms and stir-fry for 2 minutes. Add the celery, pepper and bamboo shoots and stir-fry for 3 minutes. Add the cabbage, bean sprouts, chestnuts and spring onions and stir-fry for 2 minutes. Stir in the soy sauce and sugar, remove from the heat and leave to stand for 2 minutes. Turn into a colander and leave to drain. Place a few spoonfuls of the filling mixture in the centre of each spring roll skin, fold up the bottom, fold in the sides, then roll upwards, enclosing the filling. Seal the edge with a little flour and water mixture then leave to dry for 30 minutes. Heat the oil and fry the spring rolls for about 10 minutes until crisp and golden brown. Drain well before serving.

Serves 4

45 ml/3 tbsp groundnut (peanut) oil

5 ml/1 tsp salt

2 slices ginger root, minced

450 g/1 lb mixed vegetables such as sliced bamboo shoots,

blanched bean sprouts, broccoli florets, sliced carrots,

cauliflower florets, diced peppers

120 ml/4 fl oz/½ cup chicken or vegetable stock

15 ml/1 tbsp soy sauce

5 ml/1 tsp sugar

Heat the oil and stir-fry the salt and ginger until lightly browned. Add the vegetables and stir-fry for 3 minutes until well coated with oil. Add the stock, soy sauce and sugar and stir-fry for about 2 minutes until heated through.

Vegetables with Honey

Serves 4

15 ml/1 tbsp groundnut (peanut) oil

1 slice ginger root, chopped

2 cloves garlic, chopped

100 g/4 oz baby sweetcorn

2 spring onions (scallions), sliced

1 red pepper, diced

1 green pepper, diced

100 g/4 oz mushrooms, halved

15 ml/1 tbsp honey

15 ml/1 tbsp fruit vinegar

10 ml/2 tsp soy sauce

salt and freshly ground pepper

Heat the oil and fry the ginger and garlic until lightly browned. Add the vegetables and stir-fry for 1 minute. Add the honey, fruit vinegar and soy sauce and season with salt and pepper. Stir together well and heat through before serving.

Fried Spring Vegetables

Serves 4

45 ml/3 tbsp groundnut (peanut) oil

2 cloves garlic, crushed

salt

30 ml/2 tbsp soy sauce

30 ml/2 tbsp hoisin sauce

6 spring onions (scallions), chopped

1 red pepper, chopped

1 green pepper, chopped

100 g/4 oz bean sprouts

225 g/8 oz mangetout (snow peas), cut into 4

5 ml/1 tsp tomato purée (paste)

5 ml/1 tsp cornflour (cornstarch)

120 ml/4 fl oz/½ cup chicken stock

few drops of lemon juice

60 ml/4 tbsp chopped chives

Heat the oil and fry the garlic and salt until lightly browned. Add the soy and hoisin sauces and stir-fry for 1 minute. Add the peppers, bean sprouts and mangetout and cook, stirring, until they are just tender but still crisp. Stir the tomato purée and cornflour into the stock then add it to the pan. Bring to the boil and simmer, stirring, until the sauce thickens. Sprinkle with lemon juice, stir, then serve sprinkled with chives.

Marinated Steamed Vegetables

Serves 4

30 ml/2 tbsp groundnut (peanut) oil
225 g/8 oz broccoli florets
225 g/8 oz cauliflower florets
100 g/4 oz oyster mushrooms
2 carrots, thinly sliced
1 stick celery, thinly sliced
120 ml/4 fl oz/½ cup dry white wine
30 ml/2 tbsp plum sauce
30 ml/2 tbsp soy sauce
juice of 1 orange
5 ml/1 tsp freshly ground pepper
30 ml/2 tbsp wine vinegar

Heat the oil and stir-fry the vegetables for about 5 minutes then transfer them to a bowl. Add the wine, plum sauce, soy sauce, orange juice and pepper and toss well to mix. Cover and refrigerate overnight.

Place the marinated vegetables in a steamer, cover and cook over gently boiling water to which the wine vinegar has been added for about 15 minutes.

Vegetable Surprises

Serves 4

225 g/8 oz broccoli florets

225 g/8 oz cauliflower florets

225 g/8 oz brussels sprouts

30 ml/2 tbsp honey

30 ml/2 tbsp soy sauce

30 ml/2 tbsp wine vinegar

5 ml/1 tsp five-spice powder

salt and freshly ground pepper

225 g/8 oz/2 cups plain (all-purpose) flour

250 ml/8 fl oz/1 cup dry white wine

2 eggs, separated

15 ml/1 tbsp grated lemon rind

oil for deep-frying

Blanch the vegetables for 1 minute in boiling water then drain. Mix together the honey, soy sauce, wine vinegar, five-spice powder, salt and pepper. Place the vegetables in the marinade, cover and chill for 2 hours, stirring occasionally. Mix the flour, wine and egg yolks until smooth. Whisk the egg whites until stiff then fold them into the batter. Season with salt, pepper and lemon rind. Drain the vegetables and coat them in the batter. Heat the oil and deep-fry until golden brown. Drain on kitchen paper before serving.

Sweet and Sour Mixed Vegetables

Serves 4

45 ml/3 tbsp groundnut (peanut) oil

2.5 ml/½ tsp salt

2 cloves garlic, crushed

2 carrots, sliced

1 green pepper, cubed

100 g/4 oz bamboo shoots, cut into strips

1 onion, cut into wedges

100 g/4 oz water chestnuts, cut into strips

100 g/4 oz/½ cup sugar

60 ml/4 tbsp chicken stock

60 ml/4 tbsp wine vinegar

30 ml/2 tbsp soy sauce

15 ml/1 tbsp cornflour (cornstarch)

Heat the oil, salt and garlic until the garlic turns light golden. Add the carrots, pepper, bamboo shoots and onions and stir-fry for 3 minutes. Add the water chestnuts and stir-fry for 2 minutes. Mix together the sugar, stock, wine vinegar, soy sauce and cornflour then stir it into the pan. Cook, stirring, until the sauce thickens and clears.

Serves 4

30 ml/2 tbsp groundnut (peanut) oil

2 cloves garlic, crushed

5 ml/1 tsp salt

100 g/4 oz smoked bacon, diced

30 ml/2 tbsp tomato purée (paste)

30 ml/2 tbsp soy sauce

30 ml/2 tbsp honey

30 ml/2 tbsp hoisin sauce

300 ml/½ pt/1¼ cups vegetable stock

1 red pepper, cut into strips

1 green pepper, cut into strips

1 stick celery, cut into strips

100 g/4 oz bean sprouts

100 g/4 oz green peas

10 ml/2 tsp wine vinegar

Heat the oil and fry the garlic and salt until lightly browned. Add the bacon and fry until crisp. Blend together the tomato purée, soy sauce, honey, hoisin sauce and stock. Add the vegetables to the pan and stir-fry for 2 minutes until coated in oil. Add the stock mixture, bring to the boil, cover and simmer for about 20 minutes until cooked.

Water Chestnut Cakes

Serves 4

100 g/4 oz sesame seeds
900 g/2 lb water chestnuts
15 ml/1 tbsp plain (all-purpose) flour
5 ml/1 tsp salt
freshly ground pepper
225 g/8 oz red bean paste
oil for deep-frying
120 ml/4 fl oz/½ cup vegetable stock
15 ml/1 tbsp sesame oil
5 ml/1 tsp cinnamon

Toast the sesame seeds in a dry pan until lightly browned. Mince the water chestnuts and drain off a little of the water. Mix with the flour, salt and pepper and shape into small balls. Press a little bean paste into the centre of each one. Coat the cakes in sesame seeds. Heat the oil and deep-fry the cakes for about 3 minutes then remove from the pan and drain. Pour off all but 30 ml/2 tbsp of oil from the pan then return the cakes to the pan and fry over a low heat for 4 minutes. Add the remaining ingredients, bring to a simmer and simmer until most of the liquid has been absorbed. Transfer to a warmed serving plate and serve at once.

CPSIA information can be obtained
at www.ICGtesting.com
Printed in the USA
BVHW060945290321
603631BV00002B/288